Winter Friends

To dear Christy,
who loves the snow
—M.Q.

To my mom,
who bundled me up in itchy chunky knits
—H.N.

Winter Friends

by Mary Quattlebaum

illustrated by Hiroe Nakata

A DOUBLEDAY BOOK FOR YOUNG READERS

After the Storm

I cold-toe creep
to the window to see
the covers heaped
on each bare tree,
piled high and deep
on bin and street.
The city's tucked up,
fast asleep.
Shhh.

In violet slippers
and pink-striped robe,
dawn peeks at the world
in its white nightclothes,
smooths the sheets,
and lets it sleep.
Shhh.

But far off—*brrr.*
Here comes the plow,
LARGE and LOUD.
Here comes the plow,
crowding the snow,
breaking the hush
like a clock alarm
that just won't shush.
BRRR.

Clean Laundry

O

mountain

steep-sloped

meadow-sweet snow-peaked.

I leap! And land in a warm heap.

My Mama's Whistle

Sweet breeze
twittery twee
my mama's whistle
waltzes me

under the table,
over the chair,
swirling my boots,
twirling my hair.

Hear it fly?
Lullaby
with wings.
My mama's whistle
is a kiss that sings.

Lost and Found

What's that splotch
against the frost?
An ink-blue dot?
One mitten, lost.

Out there, somewhere,
a cold hand hides,
a numb thumb seeks
what I have spied.

Mitten, mitten,
dropped in snow,
who will I find?
Which way should I go?

Tracks

Those marks, so deep and clear,
seem to say,
Follow here.

Those prints, all in a line,
seem to spell,
The mitten's mine.

Winter Breath

Ghost horse,
all wispy mane
and misty tail
and hooves so fleet and fine—
you rise
silently
before my eyes.

Wind seeker.
Quick leaper.
Fog gallop, away you fly.
Ghost horse,
you never fall
but slip,
when I close my mouth,
into your warm, dark stall.

Icicle Piano

ting tong
That long
instrument
glittering
under
the eaves
keeps
losing
ping
keys.

plip plop
They drop
softly
on mailbox,
loudly
on rock.
PLOCK

Each
note
rings
clear
ting
fingered
by wind,
falling
on
dazzled
ear.

CLOSED

Snow Angel

A gown of lace,
one crooked halo,
two vast wings.
Who rested in this quiet place?
What spirit rose?
Only silent snow now knows.

I lay me down
and gently trace
each graceful curve.
I trace and trace the snowy flight,
the absent face.
How perfectly I fill the space.

Greeting

My "hi" hangs white.
I stop and stare.
His shyly waving
hand is bare.

And when I help
him with his sled,
four mittens pull:
two blue, two red.

Mrs. Malley's Dog

A tassel topped with eyes,
two bows, and one black nose,
he snuffles the walk
and furiously yops
as we go sliding past the shops.

Does his yip-yap ever stop?

Mrs. Malley plops
him plumply in her lap—
and there he hops,
yip-yip-yap-yop,
a frantically excited mop.

Baby Jo

Twiggy arms,
three balls of snow—
we make a doll
for Baby Jo.

She laughs and tries
to pat its hair
but she's bundled fat
as a polar bear.

Still, Jo can poke
her tongue to take
a first-time taste
of floating flake.

Squirrel

Where did it go—
the fat nut tucked
in the hidey-hole?

Here? Here?
He digs and darts.
His brush-tail bristles.

Cher-er-er.
He scolds and scolds
this mean white stuff
that stole his snack
and chills his toes.

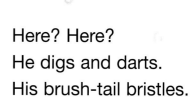

Cardinal

The bush, white-spangled
and wrapped just so . . . a red flash—
there!—the perfect bow.

Sledding

Starting slow
crouching low
we grip
the creaky sled
and go
down
down
down
whhoooaa
slipping
sliding
riding
the slope
like a wild
swan
swooping
speeding
taking
the stinging
wind
and gliding
sleek
and sure.
We are light.
We are pure
flight.

And when it ends
the hill calls out:
Again! Again!

Pigeons

Twelve plump clouds touch gently down.
They bow and peck the crumbs we threw
like tasty rain and rise again
to merge with sky's huge puffs, gray-blue.
See their tracks like scattered stars?
Hear their far-off thank-you coo?

Yellow Crocus

Spry
sprocket,
up from
earth's
dark pocket
you spring,
one
slim
sprig,
petals
wheeling
summer-
bright
under
pale
sun.

Recipe for a Party

Take one pan, shiny
as the moon.
Stir in milk
with a silver spoon.

Add some cocoa,
dark and sweet.
Blend it over
gentle heat.

Soon steam will rise
and quickly send
an invitation
to each friend,

who sniffs and smiles.
When you hear knocks,
put out mugs.
Serves lots.

Listen!
The wind
is
whispering
a thousand
tiny
promises.

Acknowledgments

Thank you to the D.C. Commission on the Arts and Humanities, and the National Endowment for the Arts, for a grant in support of my creative writing during the time these poems were written. And thanks for good fellowship and cheer over the years to wonderful neighbors Chris Bartolomeo and Dan Murphy, Ruth and Mark Walkup, Shelley and Jeff Summerlin-Long, Rachel Young and Tony Manzo, Bill Harrison and his birds, and Willie Burke and his cat, Prissy.

A Doubleday Book for Young Readers

Published by
Random House Children's Books
a division of
Random House, Inc.
New York

Doubleday and the anchor with dolphin colophon are registered trademarks of Random House, Inc.

Text copyright © 2005 by Mary Quattlebaum
Illustrations copyright © 2005 by Hiroe Nakata

Visit us on the Web! www.randomhouse.com/kids
Educators and librarians, for a variety of teaching tools, visit us at www.randomhouse.com/teachers

LIBRARY OF CONGRESS CATALOGING-IN-PUBLICATION DATA

Quattlebaum, Mary.
  Winter friends / by Mary Quattlebaum ; illustrated by Hiroe Nakata.
    p. cm.
  "A Doubleday Book for Young Readers."
  ISBN 0-385-74626-1 (hardcover : alk. paper)—ISBN 0-385-90868-7 (library binding : alk. paper) 1. Lost articles—Juvenile poetry. 2. Friendship—Juvenile poetry. 3. Mittens—Juvenile poetry. 4. Winter—Juvenile poetry. 5. Children's poetry, American. I. Nakata, Hiroe, ill. II. Title.
  PS3567.U282W56 2005
  811'.54—dc22

                              2004030937

The text of this book is set in 14-point Helvetica Neue.
Book design by Trish Parcell Watts
MANUFACTURED IN CHINA
October 2005
10 9 8 7 6 5 4 3 2 1